Written by Dana Holyfield

Honey Island Swamp Monster Documentations

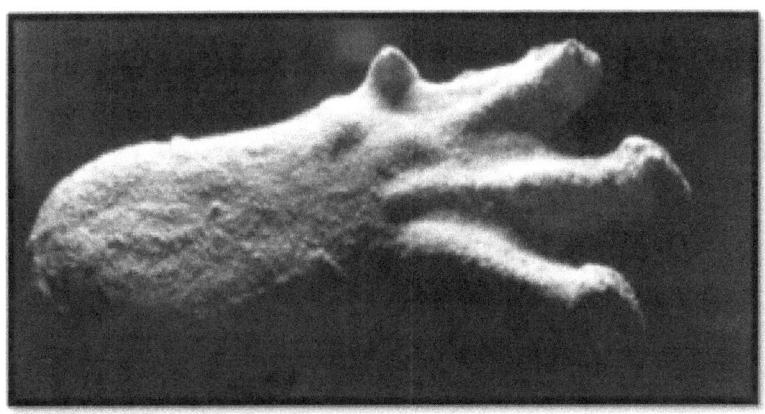

1

My name is Dana Holyfield. I am the granddaughter of the legendary swamp monster hunter, Harlan Ford, who was the first eyewitness to recount his encounter with what has since become renowned worldwide as the Honey Island Swamp Monster. I was raised in Slidell, Louisiana, in a picturesque rural area I affectionately dubbed "The Riverhood," enveloped by the West Pearl River, which meanders to the very heart of the Honey Island Swamp. Our family

2

possessed a houseboat situated upriver, accessible solely by boat, where we would retreat from civilization for the weekends. We would engage in fishing and hunting, preparing our catch, all while remaining vigilant for the Honey Island Swamp Monster, who might wish to join us for dinner—uninvited, of course. The eerie sounds echoing across the moonlit river were a customary aspect of our lives. Not that one ever truly acclimatizes to the vulnerability of a swamp; rather, we learned to embrace the fact that the swamp is an enigmatic and occasionally perilous realm, and we never underestimated the creatures that inhabit it.

1

Dana Holyfield

Honey Island Swamp is one of the most pristine and unspoiled wetlands in the United States, situated in Southern Louisiana on the northeastern flank of Saint Tammany Parish, extending approximately twenty miles in length and seven miles in width.

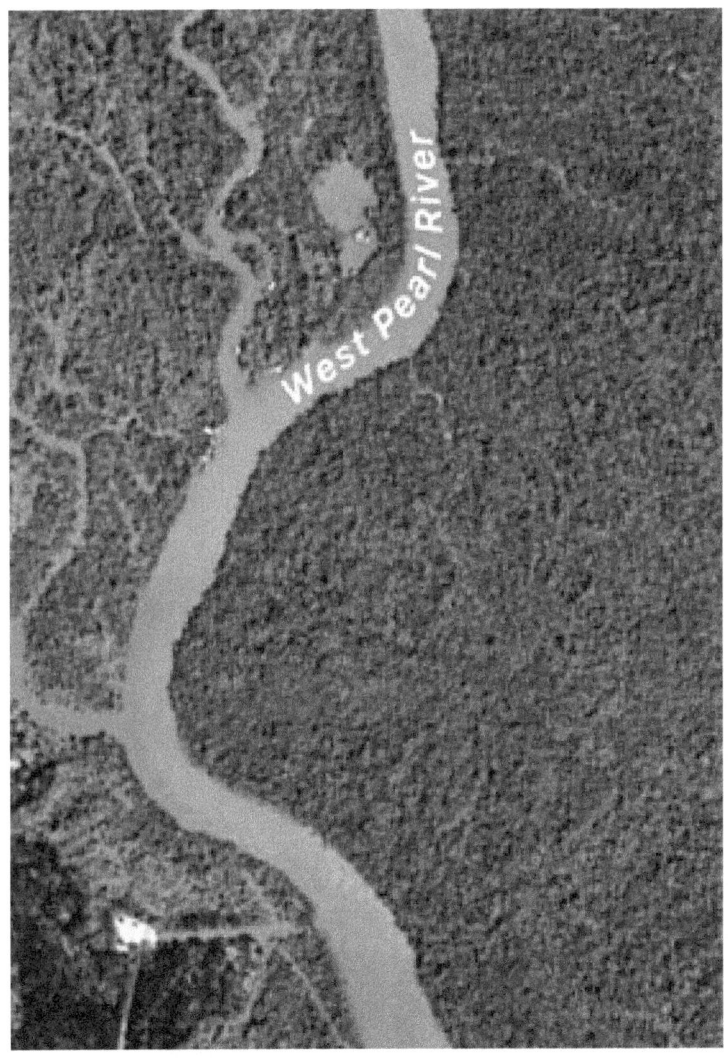

Honey Island Swamp derives its name from its status as a natural haven for honey bees. The dense undergrowth and towering cypress trees, adorned with cascading Spanish moss, provide an ideal camouflage for a myriad of swamp inhabitants. Numerous legends have emerged from this enigmatic swamp, including tales of concealed pirate treasures buried within the hollowed trunks of cypress trees, as well as ancient Indian mounds and burial sites that have unsettled unwitting trespassers, who claim to have encountered ethereal spirits. However, the most renowned legend associated with this locale is that of the Louisiana Honey Island Swamp Monster, a tale immortalized by my grandfather, Harlan Ford.

6

In my early twenties, I embarked on a journey far removed from the enchanting Louisiana swamp, traveling to Los Angeles to pursue a career as a fashion model, actress, and screenwriter. Yet, I have never forgotten the swamp's mystical allure, nor the captivating tales that reside within its depths. Among these stories, the most unforgettable is that of my grandfather's encounter. I have always believed in the authenticity of his narrative, particularly when he gazed intently into my eyes during my childhood, around the age of ten, and proclaimed, "I don't rightly care what anyone else thinks. I know what I witnessed, and you would do well to exercise caution when you venture back out there."

7

After spending eight years in California, I found myself engulfed by a profound sense of homesickness, prompting my return to my roots. So, I packed up and headed back to the Louisiana swamp. I resolved to continue writing about the subjects I knew best: the intricate tapestry of swamp life, the art of swamp cooking, and the enigmatic swamp monsters. During numerous boat excursions with family and friends, I encountered a host of locals who recounted their own encounters with the legendary creature. However, it was my personal experience, which you can explore in this book, that compelled me to pursue my grandfather's research.

8

Armed with my video camera, I documented these boat rides, and when the opportunity arose to capture an interview with an unsuspecting eyewitness willing to share their story on camera, my amateur, no-budget documentary film was born.

9

HARLAN FORD

The Original Swamp Monster Hunter

In 1963, Harlan Ford and his hunting companion, Billy Mills, were transporting provisions to their campsite in the enigmatic Honey Island Swamp of Louisiana when they encountered an entity that would haunt them for the remainder of their lives.

They were traversing a path they had meticulously cleared to facilitate their journeys between their campsite and the main river. It was there that they beheld an intriguing sight ahead in the clearing. Initially, they presumed it to be a wild hog foraging in the earth. However, upon hearing their voices, it rose to an upright position and turned to confront them. Standing at least seven feet tall, it possessed long, disheveled, muddy hair that cascaded around its face. It

11

boasted broad shoulders and elongated, sinewy arms. Its loins were muscular, adorned with shorter, unkempt hair. However, it was its large amber eyes that most startled them, holding their gaze for a fleeting moment before it turned and vanished into the thicket. The seasoned outdoorsmen were rendered speechless, for it was unlike any creature they had ever encountered in the swamp. In fact, it appeared too anthropomorphic to be classified as an animal. Yet, it undeniably was not human.

12

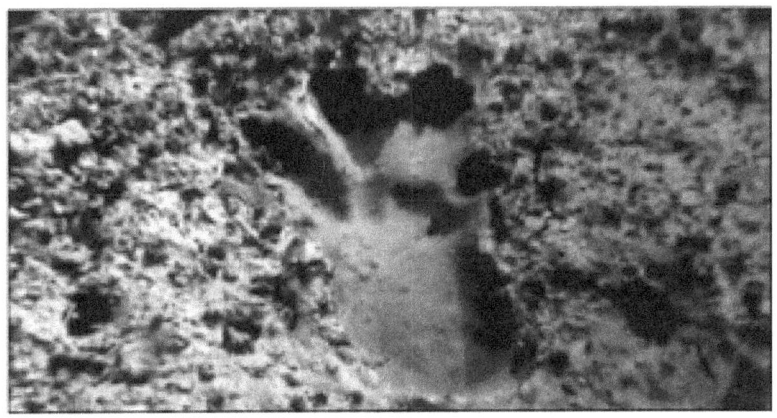

Over the years, numerous hunters and anglers have recounted encounters with this enigmatic legendary creature. However, it was Ford who emerged as the inaugural eyewitness to document his experience in 1974, after discovering tracks near a watering hole in the very vicinity where he and Billy Mills confronted the beast.

Harlan Ford and Billy Mills had encountered analogous tracks when they stumbled upon several deceased wild boars, their throats gruesomely slashed open.

Blood was spattered across the foliage where the wild boars were slain. Normally, animals pursue other creatures for sustenance. However, this instance resembled a territorial execution.

13

There are few species in a Louisiana swamp that possess the size and strength necessary to subdue the formidable wild boar, which are equipped with razor-sharp tusks capable of shredding even the most resilient of materials.

If an alligator were to have committed the act, it would have undoubtedly dragged its quarry back to its lair. Furthermore, alligators typically remain in close proximity to aquatic environments. Some of the feral hogs, however, were situated deep within the forest. Additionally, other predators, such as bobcats, generally do not abandon their prey to decay in the underbrush.

Thus, the sole conclusion that Harlan and Billy arrived at regarding this brutal massacre, motivated by territorial disputes, was the formidable creature they had previously encountered in the same vicinity.

14

Ford returned to the vicinity with plaster of Paris to create castings of the tracks, which he subsequently presented to a Wildlife and Fisheries Agent, Alvin Frierson.

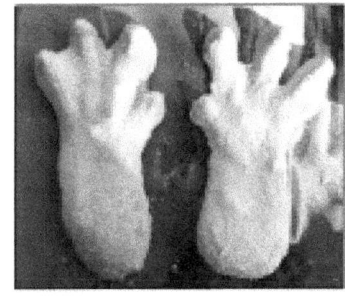

The tracks exhibited characteristics suggestive of clawed, potentially webbed toes, accompanied by a distinctly human-like arch and heel. Ford subsequently presented the castings to the Zoology Department at Louisiana State University, where they too were unable to ascertain their origin. However, they refrained from dismissing either the tracks or

15

Ford's observation, acknowledging that the mere absence of scientific recognition does not negate the potential existence of phenomena yet to be discovered.

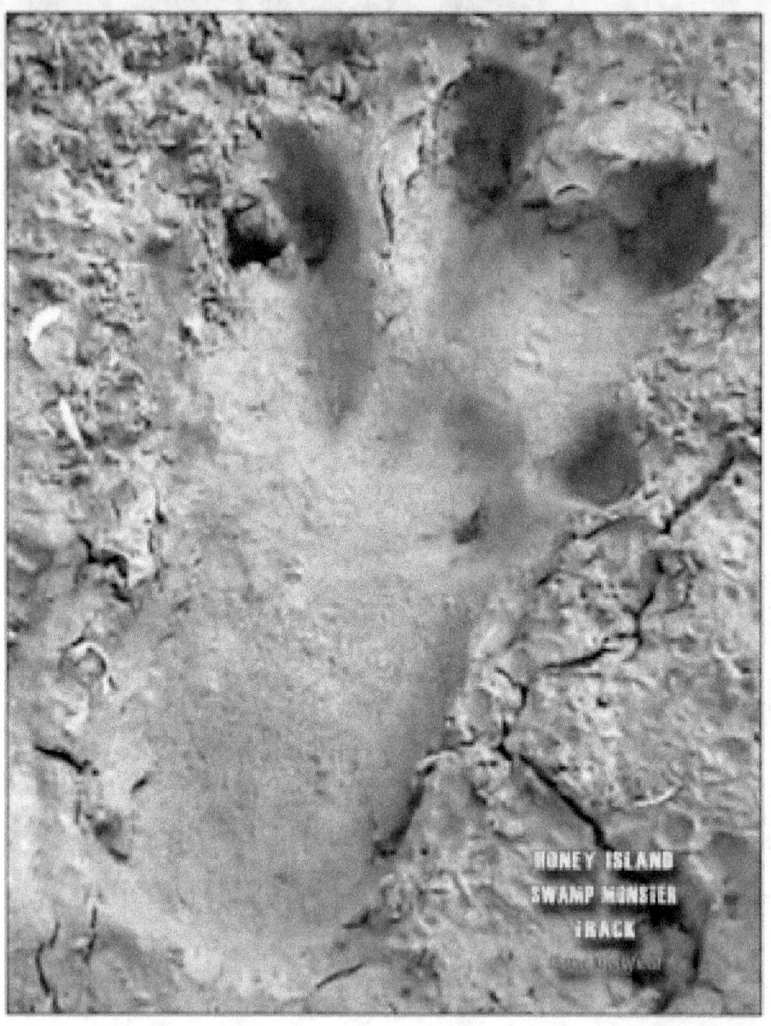

Something of this nature could endure and remain concealed within the expansive depths of this primordial swampland, which is dense with verdant vegetation and foliage. It encompasses a vast expanse that is largely uninhabited by humans, save for its peripheries. The swamp teems with an array of edible flora, such as palm hearts and lily roots. Additionally, the area boasts a rich diversity of wildlife and fish, rendering it unnecessary for a creature of its size and characteristics to venture beyond the swamp in search of sustenance.

17

Dana Holyfield

In 1975, Harlan Ford was interviewed by the illustrious Frank Davis—yes, the very same renowned Frank Davis who captivated audiences on WWL TV with his culinary prowess and hosted their esteemed fishing program. The piece was entitled "That Thing in the Swamp.".

It wasn't long after that before pranksters seized the opportunity to instigate further controversy. My Uncle Perry Ford recounted a sign posted at the boat launch that proclaimed, "Creature Season Open." Subsequently, the local Game Warden discovered a man wading backward out of the river, with a pair of tracks affixed to his shoes.

Following Harlan Ford's appearance on the national television series "In Search Of," hosted by Leonard Nimoy, a fervor for Swamp Monster hunting ensued. Monster Hunters converged from across the nation, armed and dangerous. Ford harbored concerns that someone might sustain injuries in the pursuit of capturing the creature. He was apprehensive about the possibility of one hunter inadvertently shooting another. Additionally, there were the practical jokers and skeptics who dismissed the phenomenon as an elaborate ruse. Consequently, Harlan Ford chose to bide his time as the frenzy subsided, refraining from making any further reports. However, this was not to be his final encounter with the elusive Honey Island Swamp Monster.

Harlan Ford persisted in his quest to unravel the mysteries surrounding the elusive creature. He dedicated numerous years to the pursuit of compelling evidence. His research, however, came to an abrupt halt in 1980 when he suffered a catastrophic heart attack and subsequently passed away. Yet, the legend he ignited did not fade into obscurity. In particular, the discovery of an 8mm film among his possessions, ominously labeled "Honey Island Swamp Monster," reignited interest in his findings.

20

THE 8MM FILM EVIDENCE

While producing my documentary film, my grandmother unearthed a collection of wildlife films that my grandfather had meticulously recorded many years prior. Among the various reels labeled "Gator," "Turkey," and "Deer," one film reel bore the intriguing title "Honey Island Swamp Monster." She mentioned that she was uncertain of its contents but graciously offered it for my research endeavors, should I wish to utilize it. Consequently, I inquired whether she still possessed the antiquated movie projector.

Our cousin had borrowed it to view nostalgic home movies and had replaced a malfunctioning bulb. She returned it, and we meticulously threaded the film, projecting it onto the kitchen wall. The film's perspective began with a journey upstream in a boat. Subsequently, Harlan Ford ascended into a tree-blind. From this vantage point, the camera's viewpoint swept across the wooded landscape. We were astounded to witness what appeared to be a substantial, hairy bipedal creature traversing the swamp on two legs before it vanished behind the dense foliage.

We abruptly came to the realization that Harlan Ford may have garnered more insights about this enigmatic creature during the remaining years of his life than any of us previously comprehended.

The 8mm film has since been scrutinized by several experts who assert that it is genuine footage rather than a fabrication. The digitized frames extracted from the film reveal a sloped neck and elongated arms.

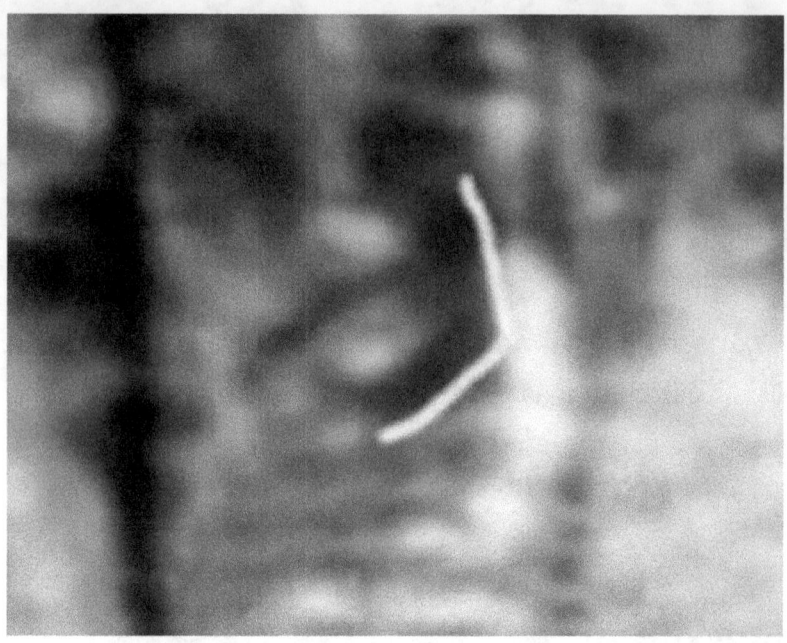

Many have pondered why Harlan Ford chose not to publicize the film. My grandmother suggested that it was likely due to the reactions he encountered when he presented the tracks in 1974. Harlan Ford was concerned that someone might venture into the swamp with the intent to harm the creature or, inadvertently, injure an innocent bystander. He certainly wished to prevent any injuries or fatalities resulting from a case of mistaken identity while attempting to hunt down the Honey Island Swamp Monster. Harlan was uncertain about how the creature would react to a human intruder, should they miss their intended target. Coming face to face with

24

something that bears an almost human resemblance could induce hesitation in a person contemplating pulling the trigger. At that moment, it might be too late. However, more than anything, Harlan Ford had become fixated on uncovering further truths about the creature, and perhaps he possessed knowledge beyond our current understanding, motivating him to protect it rather than harm it.

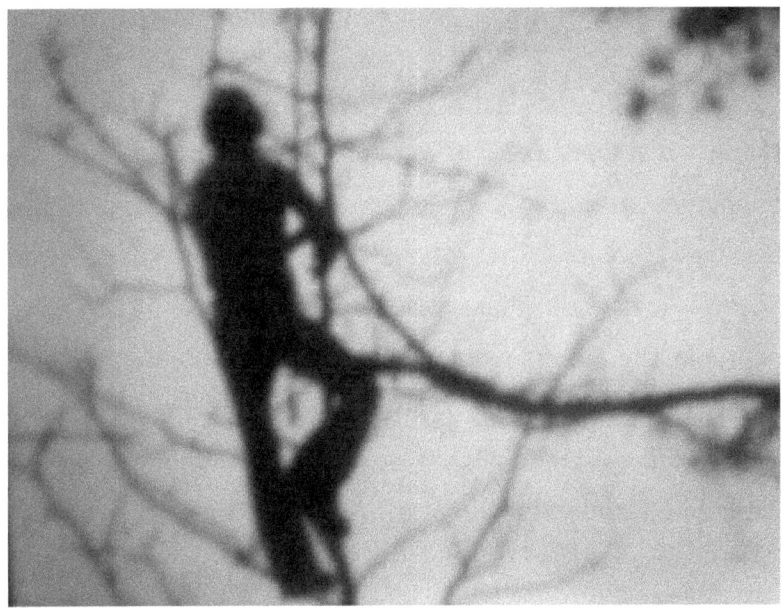

25

Why I Became a Swamp Monsterologist

Many individuals inquire whether I have experienced an encounter of my own with the legendary Honey Island Swamp Monster. Throughout my life, there have been several instances that could be deemed as such. For example, one fateful night, cloaked in darkness and an eerie ambiance in the Honey Island Swamp, the men ventured forth to inspect the catfish lines, leaving us women alone at the camp, vulnerable to whatever might emerge from the encroaching woods. It is essential to note that this occurred approximately six months after my return from California, and my urban sensibilities—though I recognize that "citifiedness" is not an actual word—had yet to dissipate in the bayou. Spending a night in a swamp, regardless of prior experiences, cannot be likened to the adage of falling off a

26

horse and simply getting back on. This is particularly true when one is acutely aware of the potential dangers that may still lurk in the shadows.

So, as we ladies gathered around the campfire that the gentlemen so graciously ignited before departing, leaving us to our solitude on the swamp island, we were suddenly startled by an

eerie howling emanating from the shadowy woods behind us. "Did you hear that?" my friend inquired.

Of course, I heard it. The sound resonated with an unsettling familiarity. Memories of childhood weekend excursions flooded back, accompanied by recollections of similar howls piercing through moonlit nights. I also recalled my grandfather's eerie encounter, along with a few other family members who had recounted analogous experiences. The dog began to growl in a low, rumbling tone, as if she were striving to alert us rather than intimidate whatever lurked beyond the shadows. She likely understood that whatever was producing the noise was not deterred by a feeble old dog like her. Then, my friend remarked on the way the dog's

27

fur bristled along her spine. A palpable sense of unease enveloped us, akin to being sitting ducks—a quintessential scenario for an encounter with the Honey Island Swamp Monster.

So, being stuck on a swampy island without a weapon on hand, nor a motorboat to escape, was not the best situation to be in. My friend pointed to an old pirogue that had been pulled up on the river bank that we could use to leave if we actually had to get gone in a hurry, even though a pirogue was not the best kind of escape method if one would be in a hurry. Plus, the paddles were in the boat with the men -- so that shot that bright idea right out of the water.

Something about being in a swamp after dusk was inherently eerie but when you begin to hear haunting creature feature sound effects echoed from behind the Cypress trees - made it even more unsettling. Especially, knowing what I knew about my grandfather, Harlan Ford's chilling sighting of a monstrous creature in this very same swamp that we were stranded in. We also knew that most dangerous swamp critters usually hunt during the cloak of night; wild hogs, panthers, bob cats, alligators, and I'm sure that applies to Swamp Monsters!

The dog barked towards the fringe of the woods but quickly retreated, her tail tucked between her legs, and scampered up onto the porch. It was at that moment we discerned that whatever had incited the dog's outburst was something she ardently wished to avoid. Thus, we concluded that it would be wise to withdraw into the cabin and secure the door until the men returned from their fishing expedition.

I propped an antiquated chair beneath the camp's doorknob, though I knew that a timeworn wooden chair would offer little resistance against a Swamp Monster should it truly wish to invade. Furthermore, the glass windows would readily yield to the force of shattering.

As we sat in contemplative silence within the confines of the camp, the only sounds that graced our ears were the melodic chirping of crickets and the harmonious croaking of frogs engaged in their nightly serenade. My friend, inspired by the ambiance, drew a parallel to a recent incident she had encountered at her home, situated a few miles downriver, while she was removing clothes from the line in her backyard. She recounted a disquieting sensation, as if an unseen observer was fixated upon her. Casting a furtive glance into the swamp, she noticed a cluster of tree limbs swaying erratically. Given that the day was devoid of wind, she instinctively surmised that something substantial must have been responsible for such pronounced movement among the trees. In a state of unease, she retreated into her house and secured the door, mirroring the actions we had taken ourselves.

Then, my other friend remarked upon the peculiar tracks she had observed around the camp island. She initially speculated that they might be alligator tracks until her husband pointed out that alligators possess more toes and typically leave a slide mark behind them from their tails. Just then, something struck the wall outside, sending us into a frenzy of terror. We screamed as if our lives depended on it, and the dog barked with equal fervor. Suddenly, an

30

unsettling silence enveloped the camp. It felt as though the crickets and bullfrogs had also been cowed by whatever menace lurked outside.

My friend seized a loaded shotgun that was propped in the corner, a precautionary measure for emergencies. Confronted by the prospect of a formidable, hairy swamp monster, it was indeed an emergency, and a loaded shotgun might be our only recourse against such a creature, should the need arise. Then, we heard another sound but this time it was a motor boat. Maybe it was the men returning from their fishing trip. But the boat kept on going down river. There went our only hope to survive – at least that's what it felt like at that moment. We attempted to convince each other that the noise we had heard was probably a rotted tree limb that broke off and fell onto the tin roof.

The dog finally settled down, though she kept her ears perked, listening and every now and then her hair would rise on her back again. I suddenly began to worry that the men may burst through the door playing a trick on us and get loaded up with buckshot. I told my friend not to shoot unless she was absolutely sure that it was a Swamp Monster. Then, I thought it would be a shame to shoot if that was indeed what it was. It would have been a good time to have a

31

tranquilizer gun handy in case we didn't want to kill it. I remembered that I had a stun gun in my bag that I had bought at the Home and Garden show. But, would 50,000 bolts of electricity stop a big and hairy Swamp Monster and give us enough time to tie it up with duct tape until I could call a Cryptozoologist to come inspect it?

It is astonishing the peculiar thoughts that can arise in a state of panic. It felt as though hours had elapsed as we jumped at every insignificant sound that pierced the silence beyond.

Then, the dog resumed barking, but this time her barks were directed at the sound of another motorboat approaching the island, carrying the men who were presumably perplexed by our decision to abandon a perfectly good campfire. We elucidated the circumstances that had transpired, and naturally, they suggested that we had likely encountered a pack of wild boar traversing the swamp. They further informed us that it was fortuitous we had retreated indoors, as wild boar could pose a greater threat than a Swamp Monster. The scene would have been a gruesome tableau, for wild hogs consume every remnant, leaving nothing behind but our DNA. We were acutely aware that the men were indulging in a bit of mockery at our expense.

32

It rained torrentially later that night, extinguishing the campfire and erasing any traces that might have been uncovered the following morning. However, I discovered my inspiration during and after that eerie incident to embark on a quest to locate additional eyewitnesses who have encountered the enigmatic entity known as the legendary Honey Island Swamp Monster. I engaged with over a dozen individuals who recounted their own experiences. Subsequently, I self-published this modest volume and produced a documentary film utilizing my home video camera. While the cinematic quality was far from professional, the production team comprised solely of myself, along with a few friends and family members who graciously provided boat rides. The book and documentary piqued the interest of numerous enthusiasts within the realm of Cryptozoology. Since that time, I have received invitations to appear on various television programs, radio broadcasts, podcasts, and to speak at several Bigfoot conferences.

— with Dana Holyfield at Salt Fork State Park.

33

Harlan Ford's Wrote To Argosy Magazine

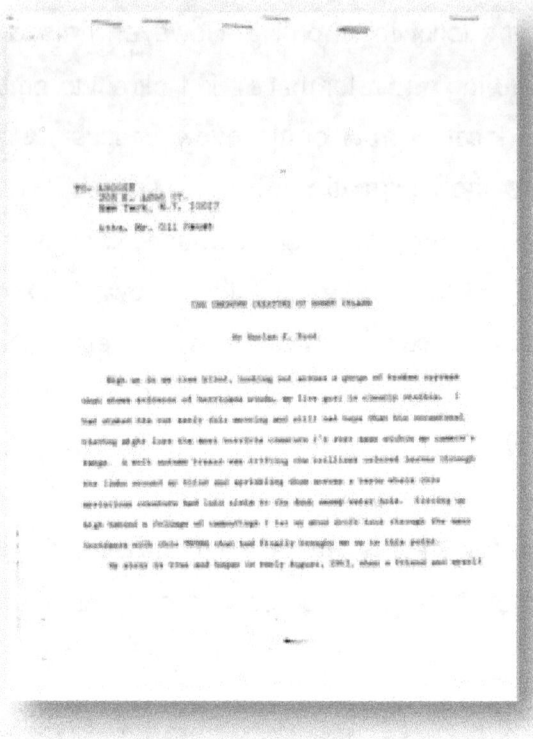

This is the original correspondence penned by Harlan Ford himself to Argosy Magazine, which was situated in New York. I am uncertain whether they ever published his narrative. I am including it unedited in this volume so that you may peruse it as well, for when a tale is recounted and reiterated over time, the story often undergoes alterations, however subtle. Thus, you now have the opportunity to engage with his account in his own words, as if it transpired merely yesterday.

34

THE UNKNOWN CREATURE

OF HONEY ISLAND

By Harlan E. Ford

High up in a tree blind, looking out across a gorge of broken cypress that shows evidence of hurricane winds, my live goat is clearly visible. I had staked him out early this morning and still had hope that his occasional blatting might lure the most horrible creature I'd ever seen within my camera's

35

range. A soft autumn breeze was drifting the brilliant-colored leaves through the limbs around my blind and sprinkling them across a bayou where this mysterious creature had laid claim to the dank swamp water hole. Sitting up high behind foliage of camouflage, I let my mind drift back through the incidents with this THING that had finally brought me up to this point.

36

My story is true and began early August 1963, when a friend and myself first encountered the creature at close range in the dense Honey Island Swamp located in St. Tammany Parish of Louisiana. The real rough part of this swamp is formed by the West and East Pearl rivers, Wilson's and Bradly's slough, bordering one of the most treacherous swamps in the country.

37

Bill and I like the satisfaction of having built a camp in this remote area because fish and game are abundant with very little infringement from other hunters. While flying a few years before, I had located the campsite between these rivers, so Bill and I used compass bearings to blaze our trail around old lakes and bayous. With the use of two boats located at key points, it was possible to walk most of the way through swamp trails to the camp. At various times we would pack our supplies into our river site, and that was the case the early August morning when we first encountered the creature. We were walking fast with a heavy load when we saw the hind quarters of what appeared to be a large animal standing on four legs in the trail. We were used to seeing all sorts of known animals in this swamp area, but as we approached within twenty feet, Bill exclaimed in a loud voice, "What the hell is that thing?"

The creature had evidently failed to hear us approaching up the trail, but at the loud sound of Bill's voice, it swung around and faced us.

Its loins were slender, while the chest and shoulders were tremendous. The head and face had a square appearance and the entire body was covered with short and dingy gray hair. The head had long, wild hair that almost touched the ground. This thing glared at us in a ferocious manner for only a split second, then rose up and ran on its hind legs, disappearing over a mound of briers and brush.

39

It was about seven feet tall and would weigh approximately four hundred pounds. Momentarily stunned, Bill and I dropped our supplies and ran to an opening in the woods in anticipation of getting a shot at it, but it completely vanished like a ghost. We searched the area close hoping to find its den or tracks, but we found nothing. This was our first and last daylight encounter, but over the past years, many incidents have occurred during dusk and night hours with this creature that resembles something out of a midnight horror movie.

Months later, one cold winter day while duck hunting around a lake in the area, another incident occurred. Moving softly through the brush and fallen leaves we were following the water's edge when we found a dead boar with its throat torn out and deep scratch marks all over its body. It was about twenty yards from the lake's edge and showed signs of having been killed days before. We hadn't gone far when we found another hog that had been killed earlier in the same identical way. Puzzled about these strange killings, we kept on moving south along the lake looking for ducks. Less than fifty yards farther, we noticed ripples on the water's surface rolling out from under a huge oak that hung over the lake. Knowing wood ducks feed on fallen acorns at the water's edge, the ripples were a sure sign ducks were there. We started crawling closer on our hands and knees to a point that would provide a clear shot but found the ripples were not made by ducks, but instead by another boar. The only difference was, even though it had been torn apart like the others, it was still alive. The dying boar was at the water's edge with just its hind legs in the lake and would kick in a convulsive manner every few seconds, causing the ripples on the water. Blood was splattered all over the bushes and leaves around a ten-foot area indicating a fierce battle of life and death had just taken place.

We wondered what kind of creature would do this just for the pleasure of killing and leave its prey lying in the woods. After seeing this, the ducks didn't seem that important anymore and we quickly vacated the lake area.

Occasionally we would take friends into our camp on hunting and fishing trips. Soon most of them heard of the creature but since it has run from us on sight and was apparently afraid of humans, no one really gave it much thought. Some even passed it off as a figment of our imaginations.

42

One friend who did just that was J.H., however he was yet to be converted. Late one afternoon, six of us were fishing down the West Pearl River, using two boats, when Bill's motor started running hot because of a busted water pump. This caused me to start boating the men back up the swift river in pairs after dark. On the first trip I had let two men off to get a fire started and was returning downstream when my head light spotted the creature standing on a bluff, overlooking the river. The water at this point was extremely swift and full of snags. I kept my light focused ahead, but each time I flashed it back up for an instant, I could see It brazenly standing there watching me. To attempt a shot in this snaggy, turbulent water, might result in a sunken boat, and two, the distance was very great.

When I reached the men waiting on the sand bar below, I began telling them what I had seen on the bluff.

J. H. hollered, "Let me have that gun of yours and I'll go back up there and shoot that big booger for you boys." Taking my model 870 magnum loaded with three shells and a flashlight, J.H. started back up the river's edge where I had spotted the creature only minutes before. Picking up the rest of the men, I started back up the river to the camp but before reaching it, we heard a deep woods echo, the sound of my gun exploding, and then a minute later, another shot.

43

Returning downstream, J.H. was waiting at the river's edge, frantically waving his flashlight. He had jumped off the bluff and was really excited when picked up. Back at the camp, he related how he had spotted this thing in the woods and had fired at it. Thinking it was down, he went deeper into the woods expecting to find the creature dead, but when he didn't find it, he began shining his light all around and saw a pair of glaring eyes approaching him from the rear. He fired a second shot at point blank range and then realizing there was only one shell left, ran for the bluff of the river.

The next morning, we went back in the woods, looked for signs of blood, but found none. What we did find was that J.H.'s second shot had hit dead center of the big oak tree.

The following spring, my son-in-law and a friend were hunting wild turkeys one evening behind the same old lake where wild hogs were slaughtered. Hearing a gobbler fly up to roost at sundown, they waited in the swamp until dusk before moving out, intending to return the next morning before daylight and get under him. When they reached camp after dark, they said they heard the creature cry out up the lake and something had followed them in the dark woods back to the river where their boat was tied. Needless to say, that gobbler made out fine since both men decided to hunt an area across the river the next morning.

44

I have hunted and fished the Honey Island for the past twenty years and believe the range of this mysterious creature is relatively small. I think it is also predominately a night prowler. Most of all encounters have been at dusk, or night, and all within a two square mile area of the swamps, lakes and bayous that surround the camp.

Still another incident occurred when a friend of ours returned to camp late one evening, and being the first one in, proceeded to gather wood and start a fire. When the woods were dark, he saw something standing in the brush staring at him. The creature moved its head from side to side. It stood straight up tall on two legs and it was huge. Our friend grabbed his gun and shouted at it only to see it disappear in the darkness of the woods. He said he could have shot it — but for an instant he thought it might be human.

A similar incident happened to my son, Perry and his wife while at the camp. At dusk both heard a horrible animal sound crying out from the lake south of camp. Armed only with a light gage gun and not wanting to alarm his wife, Perry passed the sound off as nothing. When the creature cried out again a second time, much closer to the camp, Perry began building a fire.

45

The creature approached the camp sight, circled the fire, growling and crying out in a horrible animal sound. My son and his wife spoke of it being so close at times in the dark shadows; they could actually hear it breathing. Perry, who has been used to swamp sounds and the call of wild animals all of his life, had never heard anything like this before. It finally left and traveled west toward another lake behind the camp.

Since then, we have tried to trail dogs in the swamp to lead us to the creature and track him down without success. On one camping trip, we took only one ferocious dog that would fight anything. In the middle of the night, this dog became afraid of something in the woods and frantically began whining and scratching at the door of the camp. When we opened the door, he ran in, got under a cot and refused to go back out for the rest of the night. I truly believe that animals do have an acute sense of danger.

47

Early in October, 1974, we were attempting to cross the swamp in a more remote area when our path suddenly became impassable. We turned north and our compass led us into a ravine that had never been penetrated before. While crossing this gorge we noticed that it led into a maze of swamp bayous, and there we found tracks of the creature leading down to a water hole. This time we made plaster of paris cast of the thing's tracks. Some of the foot prints are over ten inches long with reptile-like claws and toes, while

48

the heel and arch have characteristics of the big ape family. Members of the Louisiana Wildlife and Fish Commission, Archaeologist and leading Zoologist from Louisiana State University have examined the track castings and have been unable to identify them.

Eagle Films Inc. approached me for track castings and information with the intentions of filming a movie in the Honey Island Swamp about this unknown creature.

49

As I sit here in my tree blind, using my live goat for bait, I am aware that this creature's diet might not consist of meat. If it only makes its appearance under the cover of darkness, my camera would be rendered useless. There is the possibility; however, that it will kill the goat at any time if the creature feels that his territory is being threatened.

There are as many unanswered questions as there are cypress trees in this swamp. The one that burns my mind is—what is this unknown creature that claims the dense swamps of Honey Island for its home?

Harlan Ford
Eye-Witness
Honey Island
Swamp Monster

THE CONTROVERSY

REAL OR HOAX?

Many years ago, Ricky Holifield—(unrelated to me)—asserted that he discovered a counterfeit shoe track embedded in the mud behind my grandfather's hunting camp. This revelation incited considerable

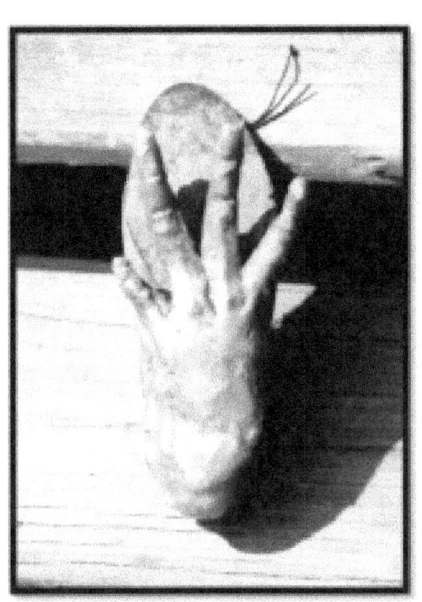

skepticism within the cryptozoology community. Numerous staunch believers transitioned to skepticism, seeking to discredit Harlan Ford and the tracks he had unearthed. Consequently, when I embarked on my documentary film, I sought out Ricky Holifield to examine the purported shoe track. Although it bore a resemblance to the tracks my grandfather had discovered, the toes appeared more akin to elongated fingers. Moreover, my grandfather's foot size did not correspond with that of this shoe. This diminutive shoe would likely accommodate a rather short individual, such as Ricky Holifield. Furthermore, if my grandfather had intended

51

to orchestrate a hoax, he certainly would not have left behind a counterfeit shoe track in the mud behind his camp.

I surmised that if it had indeed been found in the mud, it might have been left by a film crew that visited the area to interview Harlan Ford. He mentioned in his correspondence that he had provided a copy of the track to Eagle Films. I am confident he also supplied a copy to the "In Search Of" film crew. The reality is that anyone could adhere an existing track to the sole of a shoe and assert it was a hoax. A family member of Ricky informed me that they were reluctant to have an influx of individuals in their prime hunting territory searching for a Swamp Monster. Thus, they endeavored to quell the narrative. They nearly succeeded. If it was not Ricky Holifield fabricating the hoax to deter future Monster Hunters or attempting to portray my grandfather as a fool—given their contentious history over hunting grounds—then that shoe track might have originated from a film crew's prop department for reenactments on camera. This notion seemed equally plausible, as every time a film crew has approached me for an interview, they request to obtain a copy of the track, or at the very least, to borrow one to imprint in the mud for a reenactment. Alternatively, they seek a copy to discuss on camera.

I found it rather amusing that Ricky Holifield claimed he could recall the specific type of shoes my grandfather wore

52

all those years ago. I suspect many individuals sported similar styles during that era. However, I can assert one certainty: if my grandfather had indeed intended to affix tracks to the soles of shoes to traverse the swamp, he would have adhered them to a pair of rubber water boots or some other robust swamp footwear—not a fine pair of dress shoes.

Anyone could make a fake track out of an existing real track, or even sculpt it themselves with their own creative abilities. It wouldn't be that difficult to replicate the track and glue it to a pair of shoes and say it was a hoax! We know that many people don't believe that there could be a very large swamp

53

monster roaming around for all of these years without being captured or shot dead! But, look how seldom it is to come across wild animals like bob cats, jaguars, even deer that are very plentiful in a swamp. Animals can smell and usually hear a human coming from a mile away. But sometimes their luck runs out and they get seen by a fisherman or hunter who may stumble upon them unexpectedly. Just like the Swamp Monster gets stumbled upon once in a full moon.

Over the years, an increasing number of eyewitnesses have come forward with similar accounts of sightings. Surely, not everyone was fabricating a fantastical tale merely to have their names splashed across the pages of the newspaper. In fact, most of the witnesses I encountered while researching for my book and documentary film preferred to remain anonymous, fearing they would be labeled as eccentric by their skeptical neighbors.

54

JOURNALIST, H.L. ARLEDGE

I had the distinct pleasure of conducting an on-camera interview with the esteemed journalist, H.L. Arledge, during the production of my documentary film. Remarkably, he had previously interviewed my grandfather, Harlan Ford, many years ago at the inception of his journalism career. At that time, he was contributing to a daily column in The Daily Sun newspaper, crafting a piece titled "Adventures in the Unknown." The editor provided H.L. with Harlan Ford's contact information, and he reached out to him directly.

"We talked on the phone for 45 minutes. I was still in high school and an impressionable young man, and Harlan Ford was my Indiana Jones," he said. "Then, later when I was working for the Harold Vindicator newspaper, I called Harlan

55

Ford again for another interview. Then, after that, I was doing a radio show called, "Mysteries of the Unknown" and I gave him another call. I asked probing questions because I wanted to make sure we were talking about something that was real. And I felt like I got that answer. If it was a hoax, Harlan Ford didn't know about it," HL Arledge concluded.

Lloyd Pye, a distinguished authority in the realm of Alternative Knowledge.

During the production of my documentary, I had the privilege of interviewing Llyod Pye, who meticulously examined the tracks and  concluded they were authentic. "I'm certain it can climb," he remarked, scrutinizing the curvature of the foot and toes, which he asserted appeared prehensile. "It is evidently a bipedal creature that created this," he affirmed. "Much like the Little Man of the Trees."

But according to many eye-witnesses, the creature they encountered was not so little. But according to numerous eyewitnesses, the creature they encountered was far from little.

CRYPTOZOOLOGY
FRIEND,
M. K. DAVIS

To my astonishment, M.K. Davis, the esteemed cryptozoologist who once harbored skepticism regarding my grandfather's account due to the counterfeit shoe print that Ricky Holifield possessed, has transitioned into a firm believer after uncovering his own evidence in the very vicinity of Honey Island Swamp where my grandfather had his encounter. We had the opportunity to reunite in person while filming a television show alongside Chris Jericho for the Travel Channel. M.K. presented to me some intriguing new evidence that he had discovered.

More Encounters in Honey Island Swamp

There have been numerous captivating tales of the Swamp Monster shared by locals who reside in river camps and houseboats nestled within the heart of Honey Island Swamp. I surmise that if individuals spend as much time in a swamp as certain members of my family and friends do, they are inevitably destined to encounter some form of the extraordinary.

MY FATHER, DAN HOLYFIELD

My father, Dan Holyfield, was returning to our houseboat after a day of turkey hunting when the motor of his boat struck an unseen object in the middle of the Pearl River. Initially, he presumed it to be a log, until he witnessed something substantial emerge from the water and ascend onto the sandy bank. To his astonishment, it then stood upright and began to traverse towards the woods. Concerned that it might be a person in distress, potentially injured from a collision with the boat, he called out to inquire if they were alright. Yet, whatever it was continued its march, seemingly oblivious to his presence. He described it as resembling an

60

individual clad in a long trench coat, swaying rhythmically as it walked—though he later considered that it might have been long hair. He pondered what a human might be doing swimming across that section of the river at dusk, particularly given that large alligators are known to hunt at that hour. Consequently, my father maneuvered his boat closer to the sandy bank and illuminated the area with his flashlight, searching for any signs of blood. It was then that he discovered tracks, and they were unmistakably not human. They bore a striking resemblance to the three-toed, webbed footprints that my grandfather had previously encountered. Alarmed, he promptly decided to vacate the area.

My brother, Mark Holyfield, and his friend, Scott Bond, constructed a camp deep within the swamp, elevated approximately eight feet above the ground on sturdy pylons.

While camping under the stars one night, their dog began to bark fervently at something lurking beyond the confines of the camp. Suddenly, a harrowing and agonizing cry erupted from the dog, as if it were under siege. They retrieved their firearms and descended the ladder in search of their dog, whose plaintive whines echoed in the distance, growing fainter and more elusive with each passing moment.

The dog's desperate pleas for assistance finally ceased, enveloping them in an unsettling silence. They failed to discern any tracks due to the hardened terrain—there had been no rainfall for some time. However, they did observe blood splattered upon the leaves of the trees.

So, they were uncertain about what had seized their dog and spirited it away into the shadowy woods. They speculated it might have been a bobcat or perhaps a wild boar. The next time they visited that campsite, they discovered that something had ascended the ladder and had ravaged everything within, leaving a trail of destruction. Whatever entity was responsible for this seemed to be issuing a warning, conveying its desire for them to vacate the premises. Consequently, they resolved to establish a new campsite in a different part of the swamp, one that was closer to civilization.

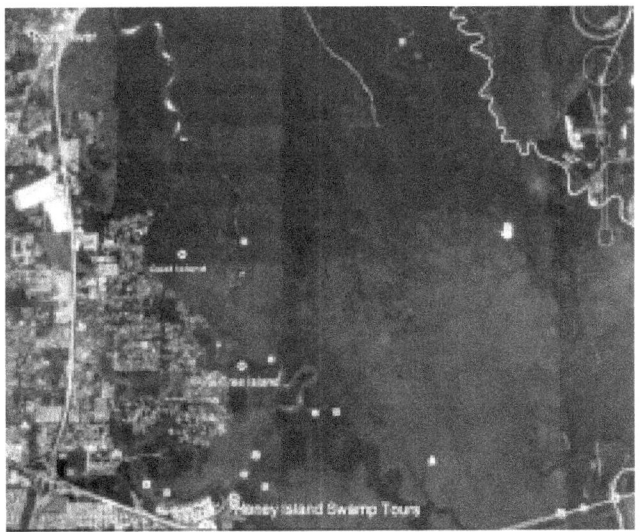

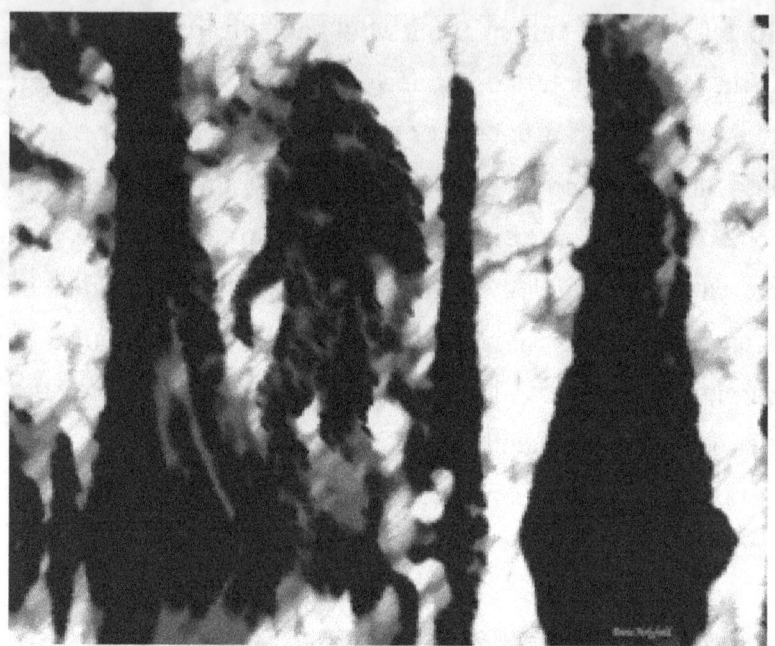

MISSING IN ACTION

In 2017, I received an intriguing message online from the great-grandson of a local individual who mysteriously vanished in the swamp. At his request, I have omitted his name to protect his privacy.

CORRESPONDENCE PAR E-MAIL

12/29/2017 6:44AM

Greetings, Dana. I have a long-lost family story that's been keep quiet. My great grandfather came home from the Pearl River one night and was saying he found a den with a monster sleeping in it and he was grabbing slugs for his gun so he could go back and kill it. He said he did not want to tell people without having this things body to back his story. He left with the bullets he came home to get and went back to the Pearl River. He launched his boat at Lock One and headed down the river to where he said he found the den. He has not been seen again. His boat was never found. Nothing. No trace of him or any of his possessions has been found to this day. My Great Grandmother and my grandmother never told anyone why he went back to the river. About 10 years ago my grandmother told me the story and told me where her daddy was headed to a den. I've went there a few times. I can tell no one goes back there. I was raised on the river and I've never been in a part of the swamp like this. There could be a city of people living back there and no one would ever know. I don't feel safe back there and it's the only place in the Honey Island Swamp that I've felt afraid. If you are interested in my findings let me know but like I said... people have walked in and never came out

JAN 2ND, 2:09PM

You accepted ********** request.

Dana

Yes I'm interested in the story. Would u be willing tell it on camera.

65

JAN 4TH, 12:24PM

I'm not sure. My Great-Grandfather's name was ***********.
I will be willing to show you where he went missing.

Dana

I remember that name. Someone told me how he also came
up missing in the swamp many years ago.
Would you be on camera to tell me the story for my next
documentary film?

When would that be? And can you black out my face? My
family wouldn't be too happy with me. They don't want
people thinking my great grandfather was crazy but I do
know something happened.

Dana

Whenever u are available and feel like doing an interview.
Maybe u can show me area on camera. It's not like old days
People take this more seriously now. Serious researchers.

END OF THAT CONVERSATION

Ted Williams

Ted Williams was a trapper and fisherman who asserted that he would often observe the creatures swimming in pairs. He remarked that they posed no threat to him, and thus he refrained from interfering with them. On one occasion, he recounted to my grandfather, Harlan Ford, that they came so close while he was seated in his boat near a riverbank that when they emerged from the bayou and shook the water from their long hair, he was doused in droplets. When the television program "In Search Of" arrived in town to interview Harlan, he directed them to converse with Ted Williams as well. A few years later, Ted Williams mysteriously vanished in the Honey Island Swamp. Authorities ultimately discovered his boat, but some who were familiar with him in the region speculated that he may have ventured too close and grown overly comfortable, leading to a fateful encounter. One of his granddaughters subsequently reached out to inform me that she believed they had located his remains, yet she was uncertain regarding the circumstances of his death. However, this information remains unverified. She did not convey confidence that they had indeed found his body, and consequently, I share her uncertainty. I distinctly recall my Uncle Perry Ford, who was acquainted with Ted Williams and closely followed the incident as an avid outdoorsman in the area, stating that while they discovered Williams' boat, his body was never recovered from the swamp.

68

Herman Broom

"*What I saw scared the life out of me,*" Herman Broom admitted. "*I was face to face with it. I didn't know whether it was man or beast.*
It had a face like a man and the body of an animal. The forward part of the face was smooth. Then it had long hair hanging around it," Herman Broom continued. "*It ran off and we tried to find it. We went up and down the levy and the Lateral Canal. Mr. Harlan Ford asked us if we had looked up in trees. We didn't look up.*"

■■

David Schutte

"We were on a sandbar swimming. As it got close to dark, something big and hairy came out of the woods and hit the water and caused a  *big splash,"* David Schutte recalls. *"I think if it was out there to hurt us, it would have probably hurt us by now. I think it is just better left alone."*

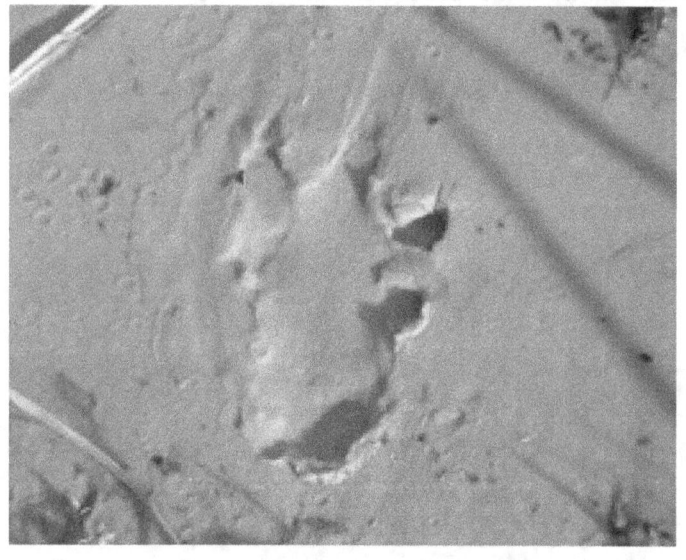

Buddy Dean Crawford

"It just leaned back against a tree. His hands supporting his head and he was just staring at us. He never moved. Just kept staring," Buddy Dean Crawford told us during his on-camera documentary interview. *"He had hair all over his body. But a face that almost looked like a man."* Buddy Dean continued. *"I was with my brother. We had been squirrel hunting around Porters River on Goat Island in the Honey Island Swamp,"* Buddy Dean stated. *"We wouldn't shoot at it because it looked too human. It never moved from that spot. It just watched us in our boat and we thought we better get on out of there."*

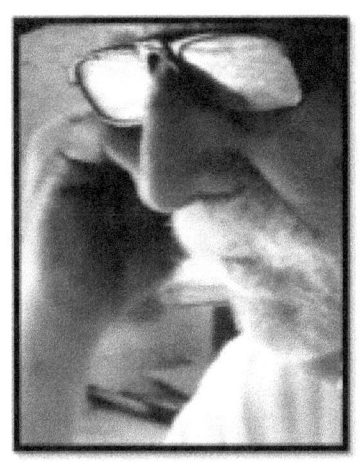

Bobby Smith

"When it looks human, but you're not quite sure it's human, you don't know whether to shoot, or run back to the house. I'll tell you the truth; it scared the heck out of me."* Bobby Smith claimed.

Jason Holburn

"We were in Debbie's Ditch, which is between East Pearl and Middle River. The moon was out so we didn't need a Q-Beam to see. Something about 50 yards away was crossing the canal. My first instinct was maybe a deer or something.

But when it was coming across, it actually looked like it was walking on two legs through the water. It got out on the other side and stood on two feet and shook its hair off then went into the woods."

Tom Broom

"We barbecued some goat on the bank next to the houseboat," Tom Broom said. "The smell was going all through the swamp. We all got on the houseboat later. All of a sudden, the houseboat went to rocking and shaking. I opened the door and seen the ass end of it going into the water."

Denty Crawford

"I was on my three-wheeler when I spotted a large animal crossing a slough and moving quickly up the levy. I thought it was a bear at first." Denty parked his three-wheeler and went on foot with his rifle after it. As he found himself in unfamiliar swamp, he heard the sound of smacking noises like something was eating something. Crawford slowly eased through the dense foliage and saw the back of something big. *"It had man-like shoulders covered with hair. But its back was flatter than rounded like a bear."* The creature was ripping tree bark off and eating the bugs from the wood. *"That was one critter I didn't want to shoot at and miss,"* Crawford admitted, knowing that one bullet may not take it

74

down if he didn't hit it just right. Crawford backed out slowly before the creature seen him or smelled him.   *"When the weeds closed in and blocked my view of that big thing, I turned and ran as fast as I could. I jumped on my three-wheeler and took off out of there. I haven't been back to that part of the swamp again,"* Denty concluded.

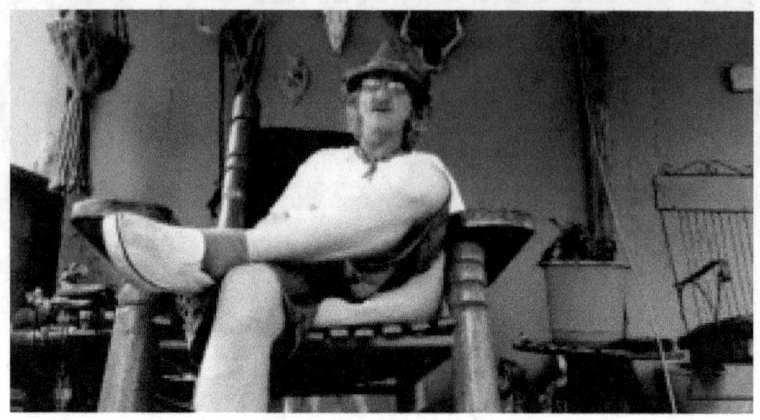

Joe Wilson

(Member of the Bogue Chitto Freedom Floaters, a group who cleans up the Pearl River while canoeing from McComb Mississippi to Slidell, Louisiana.) *"We left the mouth of the Bogue Chitto, heading to the Squirrel Camp. We stopped to camp for the night on a sandbar and built a fire. Then we started hearing strange noises over and over. In the dark you can't see what's out there. This went on all night long. So we kept the fire built up around us. When it got daylight, we walked around our campsite and found some hair."*

■■

Debra Evans Chester

"When it crossed the road and went over this fence, I wondered what in the hell was that. I could see its arm come up and it had long hair hanging down and I could see the hair on the body. I could barely see the face at the angle it was. I'm a critical care trauma ICU nurse, but this thing scared me."

Jerry Ross

"I really didn't want to tell nobody. But I was at my camp three-quarters of a mile up the river from here. My generator died. It usually runs two days on a tank of gas. So, I walked out there to look at it and see why it shut off like that. Then, I saw a huge silhouette... It was big! It had to be around 7-foot tall and it had hair all over it. It wasn't human. It had red eyes and it scared the hell out of me! So, I backed off and went back in my camp and tied my door shut with an extension cord. I looked out the window and saw the red eyes when I was shining my light. So, I shot a flare out the window and the next thing I know, it's up in the trees looking down with red eyes. It didn't try to hurt me but it stayed there most of the night. When daylight came, I left and I didn't go back to my camp for two years, until this weekend."

■■■

Steve Crawford

"We were squirrel hunting up above Bradly Slough where Bogue Chitto comes into Honey Island. We were camped on Home's Island but I always crossed over to hunt by Criers Slough. Then, when I heard all the commotion in the water behind me, I turned to look and that thing was standing about 40 to 50 feet from me looking at me. It had long black hair and stood on its hind legs. Then, it turned and ran through a briar patch. After it ran off, that was the end of hunting there for me. I left. I didn't even pick up the squirrel that I shot. I told Gene Mahann about it when I got back and he laughed at me. I said, "Look, that thing was big enough to come up in this camp and tear everything up." Then, about two weeks later, Gene said that he had to apologize to me because that thing I saw, he seen it also on a sandbar and it was huge! I said, "I know, that's why I haven't been back there."

Gary Slayden

After a rabbit hunting excursion, a group of Pearl River guys were out in the swamp by the pipeline cooking a rabbit over the fire. They heard a loud rustling in the woods. "Something big was coming through, snapping tree limbs and twigs," Gary stated, continuing to recall what took place next. To their disbelief, a large, hairy creature stepped out of the woods and moved in front of their headlights and snatched the rabbit from the fire and headed back into the woods like it didn't have a care in the world that the hunters watched it steel their dinner. They decided to get in their trucks and get out of there

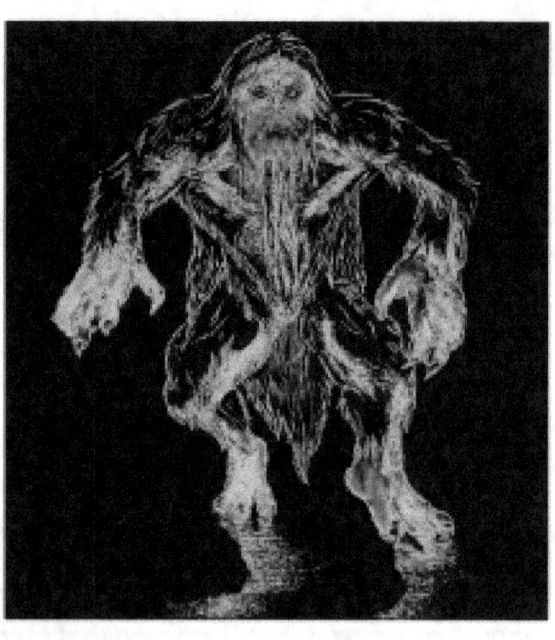

before it came back for dessert.

■■

80

Fred Lemon

"I took this gal out to my buddy's camp for the weekend. Way out there in the middle of the swamp. It started raining really bad. Then suddenly a hairy fist bursts through the glass window! That gal I was with started screaming. I looked out the window and could see a bunch of them roaming around there in the rain. So, I threw open the door and fired my shotgun at them and they scattered. We didn't sleep the rest of the night. Soon as daylight broke, we took out of there and that gal never would go back to the swamp with me again."

Terral Evans

Terral Evans *(Swamp People TV Star)* claimed that he had an encounter when he was a boy. He and his grandfather were running lines in Honey Island Swamp when they heard it nearby. His grandpa got them out of their quick, then proceeded to tell him about the creature he had also encountered prior to that day. Terral said he never saw it with his own eyes, but over the years in Honey Island Swamp, he has heard it on several occasions. He found similar 3-toed tracks and long hair in the briers nearby.

■■■■■■■■■■■■■■■■■■■■■■■■■

82

"Let me track you in here about a mile or so. I'll build you a little fire. I'll leave you with some Vienna Sausage and a Snicker Bar, and I'll come back in the morning. Then, tell me how skeptical you are," Evans told the Fox News Reporter during an interview on Hannity's America.

Another Email from An Eye-witness...

From: Terry G. <*Address Removed for His Privacy*>

To: danalouisiana@yahoo. Com

Sent: Thu, November 11, 2010 1:29:15 PM

Subject: Honey Island......

Dana, I found your email off of one of the many websites detailing your grandfather's monster story. I am glad I did. On Tuesday, November 9th myself and my stepson who is 14, decided to surprise my dad and nephew with a swamp tour. Well, it did not turn out exactly how I had planned. While on the tour boat, I had an encounter. I said nothing but froze. My dad, my stepson and nephew, along with everyone on the tour had no clue what I was looking at or that I had even saw something. I have kept it to myself over the last two days. I had to find a way to contact you. You are the only one I could tell my story too. I'm afraid to be ridiculed in any way and kept this to myself for the sake of my family. But my encounter was real, vivid and disturbing. I would like to speak to you more about this if you are interested. My stomach has been in knots for the last few days, as I am a skeptic and figured this Bigfoot stuff was a bunch of media hype, and I took the mentality that "it could never happen to

84

me." What was supposed to be a very relaxing afternoon with family turned into the most terrifying day of my life. I hope to hear from you soon, all I ask for right now is anonymity.

From: Dana Holyfield

Subject: Re: Honey Island......To: "Terry G." <*Address Removed for His Privacy*>

Date: Thursday, November 11, 2010, 8:10 PM

Thanks for writing. I would like to hear more about your sighting. What did it look like? Where was it? Was it on the ground, water or in a tree?

Subject: Re: Honey Island......
From: Terry G. <*Address Removed for Privacy*>

To: danalouisiana@yahoo.com

Date: Thursday, November 11, 2010 2:20 PM

Thank you for getting back to me Dana. Again, you are the only one I feel like I could talk to about this. As for the appearance of this thing, it was very disturbing looking as I saw the face very clearly. No hair on the face and the skin looked worn like old leather. It had huge disproportional eyes that were clearly yellowish and it was almost as if this thing had an eye disease that tinted them yellow. The hair was all over the body, gray and black in color. It was big, probably 500 lbs. and it stood about 6 to 7 Ft. tall. Some

86

other man on the tour commented on a foul, filthy, make you gag smell. The tour guide brushed it off and suggested that an animal's carcass may have been rotting or something may have been feeding nearby. It was on the bank of the swamp behind a few trees and I saw it down river by where the hunting camps are located. Please help me understand what I've seen and tell me I'm not crazy. I can answer any question you have.

Sincerely, Terry G

The area that Terry was describing is located on the East Pearl River by Indian Village boat launch. The Slidell swamp tour boats pass these camps daily. Perhaps the Honey Island Swamp Monster is becoming less intimidated by man that it was brazenly close to civilization. In the same area near Indian Village, the creature was supposedly seen digging trash out of a dumpster at night. So, it is possible that it could be seen again when someone stumbles upon him, even at the edge of Honey Island Swamp. So, keep your cameras ready if you take a swamp tour. You never know what you will encounter.

■■

If you wish to venture into Honey Island Swamp by vehicle rather than by boat, simply take Exit 5B off Interstate 59 in Pearl River, Louisiana. Proceed along this elongated, narrow thoroughfare. A shooting range diverges from this primary road. Over the years, there have been numerous sightings of the elusive creature in this vicinity. Formerly, there were walking trails meandering through the woods, but I am uncertain about the current state of the area, as it remains shrouded in ambiguity.

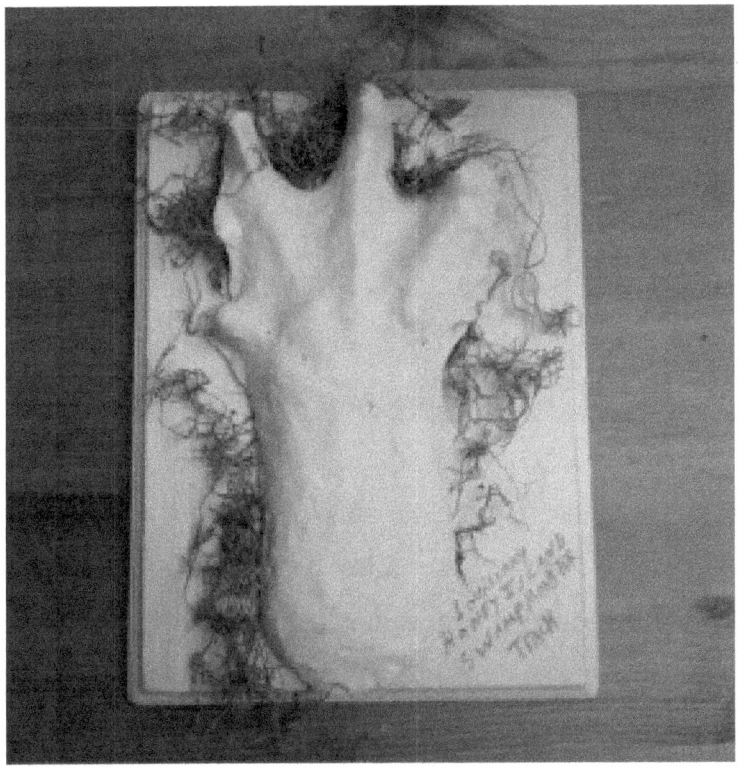

If you'd like a copy of the Honey Island Swamp Monster plaster casting to add to your cryptozoology collection, please email me for information on ordering a replica. Thanks.

Billy Mills

One of the most important interviews about the Honey Island Swamp Monster, was **Billy Mills,** Harlan Ford's co-worker, best friend, hunting and fishing buddy, who was with Harlan Ford in 1963 when they came face to face with the creature for the first time.

When I learned that my grandmother and mother were going to Texas to visit Billy Mills and his wife, Rosa, I sent my home video camera with them and begged them to get the interview if he was willing to talk on camera. It had been twenty or so years since they had seen them. Though, the lighting in the room was horrible and the background was very busy, and the "Quiet on the set" didn't work so

92

good in a busy household, they managed to get his version of what happened on that day in 1963 in Louisiana's Honey Island Swamp.

"Harlan Ford and I worked together and we hunted together," Billy said. "We would drive up to the Lateral Canal and take a boat across and walk through the woods to the camp, which was on the West Pearl, right above Bradly Slough," Billy continued. "And, on one of them occasions, we were bringing an outboard motor that we had repaired back to put on the boat that we kept in the river out there. We were also bringing some groceries and stuff for the camp. We had parked our boat and went up the levy by the Lateral Canal. We were walking through the woods to the camp in a trail we had made. And, as we rounded a bend, about twenty yards ahead, we walked upon something that was down on all fours in the bushes doing something. I never thought anything about it at first, because there are a lot of wild hogs in the swamp there. I thought it was just a big old hog. Then, it stood up! It had hair all over its head hanging down. I stopped and Harlan stopped. Just about as quickly as we saw it standing there staring at us, it disappeared behind the bushes. Both of us woodsman, hunted all our lives, broke and run to see what it was. But we couldn't find it. It could have gotten up in a tree, but we

93

never thought to look up at that time. This was in the summertime. There was a lot of foliage. Then, later on, we were squirrel hunting in the fall. We were by Bradly Slough," Mills added. "We heard something sounded like beating on a drum. A hog was squealing for dear life. I thought it had to be something big beating on that hog like that. We found some tracks. Harlan came back later on to the same area where we heard that hog and he made plaster casts," Mills concluded.

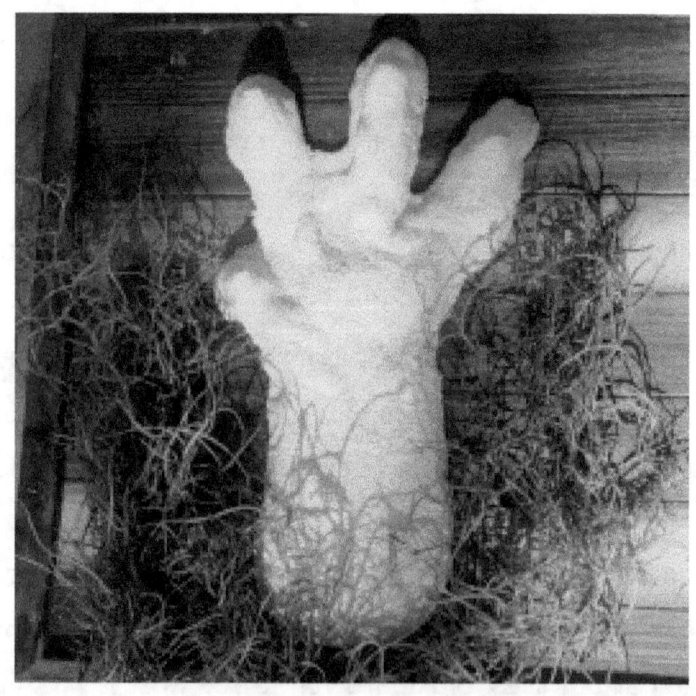

94

I Wonder Where They Came Up With This Doll?

When my daughter was a little girl and was into the Monster High Dolls, I learned that **MATTEL** had made a Monster High Doll called, *Honey Swamp, the Daughter of the Honey Island Swamp Monster.* *I was stunned, especially when I learned that the doll's description sounded a lot like me. I think they used my likeness, except I'm not green. Lol. So, of course, I bought the doll to see for myself.*

95

Here is the description of the "Honey Swamp Monster High Doll that I find interestingly familiar.

"Honey Swamp is a swamp monster, specifically the daughter of the Honey Island Swamp Monster, native from New Goreleans, Louisiana, who aspires to be a cinematographer.
That is, she's already one, and good at what she does, but she has yet to make it in Hauntlywood and beyond. She's also a girl of many talents besides photography and filming, such as cooking."

*So, let's see... I'm from the New Orleans area but moved to Hauntlywood, AKA Hollywood aspiring to be in the film business. Since I made my own documentary film, I would say I have been an aspiring cinematographer. I was also pretty good a photography. I have written cookbooks such as, "Swamp Cooking with the River People" So, that proves that I like to cook. **So, I think I should have received royalties on that doll.** Just saying.*

CONCLUSION:

Swamp Monsters, Swamp Things, the Rougarou, or whatever legendary creature is employed in your locale, serve as the focal point in numerous television programs, cinematic endeavors, comic books, literature, and various media outlets. Many individuals dismiss them as mere fabrications, conjured to inspire films, novels, and television series. However, I was astonished to discover that a substantial number of people firmly believe in the existence of enigmatic creatures lurking in the shadows behind the trees, whether within the confines of Honey Island Swamp or other marshy locales. At some juncture, these elusive beings may once again be witnessed by an unsuspecting observer, who will then possess their own tale to tell.

97

If you would like to go on a personal swamp tour into Honey Island Swamp, contact me by email so I can attempt to arrage the tour for you or get you in touch with someone who can. DHLouisiana@gmail.com

I dedicate this book to my grandfather, Harlan Ford, for his remarkable courage in sharing his story, undeterred by the opinions of others. I take immense pride in acknowledging that, in addition to being an avid outdoorsman, he was a distinguished pilot, a war veteran, and a retired official of the FAA and began building homes for people. Moreover, he was a published songwriter.. Harlan Ford cultivated numerous friendships and was held in high esteem within his community. He had connections in influential circles—such as the Louisiana Governor's Mansion, where he was frequently invited to perform at exclusive gatherings alongside his fellow musicians. While some speculate that Harlan Ford may have jeopardized his reputation by revealing his encounter with the Honey Island Swamp Monster to the media, he remained steadfast in his honesty, articulating the truth as he experienced it.

Additionally, he was a wonderful and gifted grandfather, whose inspiration propelled me to pursue a career in writing.

100